Thank you to the generous team who gave their time and talents to make this book possible:

Author
Ellenore Angelidis, Leyla Angelidis
and Worku Mulat

Illustrator
Daniel Getahun

Creative directors
Caroline Kurtz, Jane Kurtz,
and Kenny Rasmussen

Translator
Yoseph Ayalew

Editors
Mastewal Abera and
Woubeshet Ayenew

Designer
Beth Crow

Ready Set Go Books, an Open Hearts Big Dreams Project

ISBN: 979-8362226381
Library of Congress Control Number: 2022903852

Printed in Seattle, WA, U.S.A.

Published: 03/06/22

Weaving the Art People Wear

ሰዎች የሚለብሱት የሽመና ጥበብ

English and Amharic

Many beautiful Ethiopian dresses and wraps start out as cotton plants growing in a field.

ብዙ የሚያምሩ የኢትዮጵያውያን ቀሚሶችና ነጠላዎች የሚጀምሩት በእርሻ ላይ የጥጥ ተክል ሆነው ነው።

Long ago, some people learned special skills for turning cotton into cloth.

First, skilled workers take the seeds out of the puffs of cotton.

በድሮ ጊዜ ሰዎች ጥጥን ወደ ልብስ
የመቀየር ጥበብ ተምረዋል።

በመጀመሪያ ጥበበኞቹ ጥጡን ከፍሬው
በመዳመጫ ይለዩታል።

They carefully pull those white clumps in all directions until they are fluffy little pillows.

ከዚያም ትናንሽ ለስላሳ ትራሶች እስኪመስል ድረስ ጥጡን በጥንቃቄ በየአቅጣጫው እየሳቡ ያባዝቱታል።

Next, they hit a bow string—made from sheep intestine--with a tool made from a gourd. This bow does not shoot arrows. It makes the cotton soft.

በመቀጠልም በደጋን የተወጠረውን የበግ አንጀት በቅል እየመቱ ጥጡን ይነድፉታል። ይህ ደጋን ቀስት አያስፈነጥርም። ጥጡን ግን ያለሰልሰዋል።

Now it's time to spin the cotton. People have been spinning thread this way for centuries and some still do today.

አሁን ደግሞ ጥጡ
የሚፈተልበት ጊዜ ነው።
ሰዎች ከጥንት ጀምሮ
እንዝርትን በመጠቀም
ሲፈትሉ ኖረዋል፤ አንዳንዶች
አሁንም ይጠቀሙበታል።

This pot is not for cooking food. It is for cooking the cotton threads to make them even stronger.

ይህ ማሰሮ ምግብ ማብሰያ አይደለም። የተፈተለውን ጥጥ በመቀቀል ፈትሉን የበለጠ ጠንካራ ማድረጊያ ነው።

A worker winds the threads so they will be ready for weaving. Weaving is the hardest part of making cloth.

ለሽመና ዝግጁ እንዲሆን ፈትሉን አንድ ሰራተኛ በጥንቃቄ ይጠመጥመዋል። ሽመና ከልብስ ስራ በጣም ከባዱ ክፍል ነው።

A weaver uses a large wooden frame and winds the threads very quickly. He learned his art from another weaver who learned from a weaver before him, back, back to ancient times.

ሸማኔ ትልቅ የእንጨት ቢጋር በመጠቀም ክሮቹን በፍጥነት ይጠመጥማቸዋል ። ይህንንም ጥበብ ከሱ በፊት ከነበረ ሸማኔ የተማረ ሲሆን ያኛውም ሸማኔ ደግሞ ከእርሱ በፊት ከነበረው ሸማኔ ጥንት የቀሰመው ነው።

A good weaver is a skillful artist.

When it's time to make a design, the weaver needs to count and plan so that squares and lines make patterns in a rainbow of colors. It is like painting with thread.

ጥሩ ሸማኔ የተዋጣለት ጥበበኛ ነው።

ዲዛይን ለመሥራት ጊዜው ሲደርስ ካሬዎቹና መስመሮቹ በቀለማት ቀስተደመና ውስጥ ጥሩ ንድፍ እንዲፈጥሩ ሸማኔው መቁጠር እና ማቀድ ይኖርበታል። በክር ስዕል እንደመሳል ማለት ነው።

Those cotton puffs may end up as
a shawl that is worn to church,
perhaps to celebrate at a wedding
or mourn at a funeral.

ከእርሻ የተለቀመውም ጥጥ በመጨረሻ ነጠላ ሆኖ
ቤተክርስቲያን ውስጥ ምናልባትም በሠርግ ወይም
ደግሞ በቀብር ቦታ ሊለበስ ይችላል።

Every Ethiopian region is proud of its own special designs. The ancient art of weaving makes people happy and can be showed off through the clothes we wear every day.

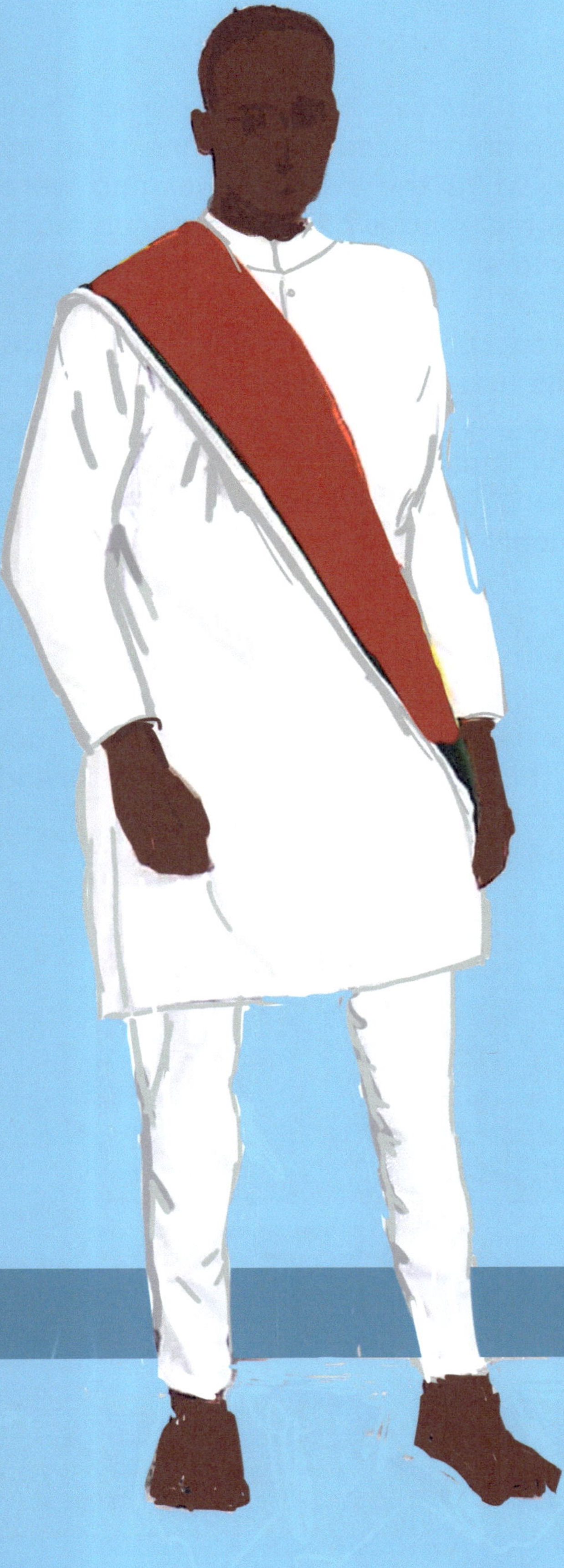

ሁሉም የኢትዮጵያ ክፍለሀገር
በራሱ ልዩ ዲዛይን ይኮራል።
ጥንታዊው የሸመና ጥበብ
ሰዎችን ያስደስታቸዋል፣ ይህም
በየቀኑ በምንለብሳቸው ልብሶች
ላይ ጎልቶ ይታያል።

About the Story

Hand weaving is an ancient art in Ethiopia. Even now, much traditional Ethiopian clothing is made this way. Spinning used to be done in many households by many classes of women, while the skills of weaving were generally taught by a father to son. The techniques haven't changed much over the years although the styles and colors have.

Authors Leyla and Ellenore Angelidis visited a community of weavers in Addis in 2014 and were fascinated by the skills and techniques of these artisans practicing a very old art form. After all, cotton has been grown in Ethiopia since ancient times. Some historians say that the first Ethiopian weavers were from Islamic and Beta Israel communities who travelled with the courts of kings and set up their looms close to noble families.

It is estimated there are now around 200,000+ hand loom weavers in Ethiopia. Today, a weaver can create one to three scarves a day depending on how complicated the design is. The Konso and Dorze ethnic groups are well-known as skillful weavers, though weavers practice their craft in just about every town in Ethiopia. We hope this Ready Set Go Book will spread support and love for an old art to children of a new generation.

About the Authors

Ellenore Angelidis is a public speaker, consultant, volunteer, lawyer, and aspiring writer. She stays busy with husband Michael and their three kids: two sons, Dimitri, Damian (who is an Open Hearts Big Dreams Junior Board member), and daughter, Leyla. Equalizing educational opportunities for children in Ethiopia is a passion that comes in part from being raised by two teacher parents and in part from raising an Ethiopian daughter. She founded and runs both OHBD and a new company L.E.A.D. (Lead Empower Activate Dream) LLC. Visiting Lake Tana and Bahir Dar has been a special highlight. Meeting and becoming friends with Eyayu Genet has led to amazing collaborations including three books. This is the first book where Eyayu Genet is also a co-author.

Leyla Marie Fasika Angelidis was born in Bahir Dar, Ethiopia and joined the Angelidis family in Seattle as an infant. She is currently in middle school and finds it unimaginable that some kids in her birth country don't get the chance to learn to read or go to school.

She has collaborated with her family to build a library in her birth town of Bahir Dar and to support other literacy projects through Open Hearts Big Dreams. She is an avid reader and aspiring writer. She has co-authored a number of OHBD Ready Set Go early reader books based on family experiences and personal interests. More recently, she is a featured spokesperson as well as helps with events and awareness building for OHBD literacy projects. Through these efforts she has learned more about her first country, language, and culture as well as positively contributed to her community in Ethiopia and in the US.

She has BIG DREAMS for herself and for kids living in Ethiopia (and around the world).

Dr. Mulat was born and grew up in a remote village called Kersole, South Wollo, Ethiopia to parents who never had the opportunity to learn how to read or to write. Drought happened often and frost frequently killed crops. Dr. Mulat vividly remembers the economic woes of his rural village. His parents were determined their children would break the cycle of poverty through unlocking the power of education. But it wasn't simple or easy. The family still needed his support, so attending elementary school needed to be balanced with farming. With his mother's strong encouragement, he excelled at school (and farming), becoming a role model to his brothers and sisters, earning advanced degrees in Biology, Environmental Sanitation and Applied Ecology. His parents, who never set foot in school, have seen all their children graduated with advanced degrees in Physics, Computer Science, Chemistry and Math.

Dr. Mulat and his family proved poverty was neither in the genes nor in the stars; rather, by taking advantage of every learning opportunity, he made poverty history for his household. His diverse life experiences have taken him to Europe, Texas, and Washington State. Dr Mulat has a strong passion to pay back to his village and others around Ethiopia through promoting literacy, innovation and education. Becoming a children's book author for kids who too rarely get to see themselves in books and sharing the rich history and culture of his birth are just some of the ways he is working to pay it forward.

About the Illustrator

Daniel Getahun lives in Toronto, Canada. He received a diploma in graphic art from Addis Ababa School of Fine Arts and Design in 1980. He now focuses on oil painting and digital painting, which can be seen on his Facebook page. He can also be contacted by email: danielgetahun1@hotmail.com

About Open Hearts Big Dreams

Open Hearts Big Dreams Fund (OHBD) was founded by Ellenore Angelidis, inspired by her Ethiopian born daughter, Leyla Marie Fasika; both are key volunteers. OHBD is a United State 501(c)(3) not-for-profit organization that believes the chance to dream big dreams should not depend on where in the world you are born. Our mission is "Inspiring and empowering youth (K-14) to reimagine their futures by providing literacy, STEAM, and leadership opportunities."

OHBD harnesses the power of collaboration. We are made up of a small number of part-time paid staff and a large number of highly motivated volunteers with advanced skills, including artistic, editorial, translation, and high-tech expertise in Ethiopia, the Diaspora and globally. Our culture of innovation means we act fast on new ideas. Since 2017, we've produced more than 700 bilingual, culturally appropriate early reader titles and a number of STEM and Model programs to increase literacy, inclusion, and leadership.

In Ethiopia, for Ethiopia; OHBD is based in the U.S. but we are committed to working with local content creators and to producing quality books in Ethiopia. Local opportunities and production builds local knowledge and capacity.

OPEN HEARTS BIG DREAMS

About OHBD Ready Set Go Books

Reading has the power to change lives, but many children and adults in Ethiopia cannot read. One reason is that Ethiopia doesn't have enough books in local languages to give people a chance to practice reading. Ready Set Go books wants to close that gap and open a world of ideas and possibilities for kids and their communities.

When you buy an OHBD-RSG book, you provide critical funding to create and distribute more books.

Learn more at: http://openheartsbigdreams.org/book-project/ or find all our books at: https://ohbd-rsgbooks.com

OHBD Proudly Prints in Ethiopia

OHBD developed our own local printing capacity and have a number of our books available to pick up in Addis. They are available for bulk purchase and we regularly donate to schools, libraries and local organizations serving kids. Please contact us at ellenore@openheartsbigdreams.org if interested in samples or ordering.

So far, we have printed and distributed (with collaborating organizations) hundreds of thousands of copies of our books in numerous languages in country.

Our goal is to get these books to all elementary students across Ethiopia.

About the Language

Amharic is a Semetic language -- in fact, the world's second-most widely spoken Semetic language, after Arabic. Starting in the 12th century, it became the Ethiopian language that was used in official transactions and schools and became widely spoken all over Ethiopia.

It's written with its own characters, over 260 of them. Eritrea and Ethiopia share this alphabet, and they are the only countries in Africa to develop a writing system centuries ago that is still in use today!

About the Translation

Yoseph Ayalew is a primary school teacher by training with a special interest in supporting the development of orphans and vulnerable children (OVC). In 2000 he founded a private school (MYFV Academy) offering kindergarten to grade 8 classes. MYFV provided a total of 54 FREE learning opportunities for orphans and vulnerable children; 15 of them funded by MYFV and 39 funded by an American NGO. In 2006, in collaboration with Volunteer Services Overseas (VSO), a UK NGO, Yoseph published his first children's book on HIV/AIDS. All books were distributed FREE to schools in Addis Ababa and throughout Ethiopia. In 2012, he published 2 books: "50 Answers to Children's Questions About HIV/AIDS" in collaboration with Ethiopia Reads, USA; and "The Loss of Innocence" in collaboration with People to People (P2P) Canada. Since 2011, Yoseph has been organizing a children's festival at the Addis Ababa Exhibition Center to celebrate the International Day of African Child.

Printed in France by Amazon
Brétigny-sur-Orge, FR

14170536R00020